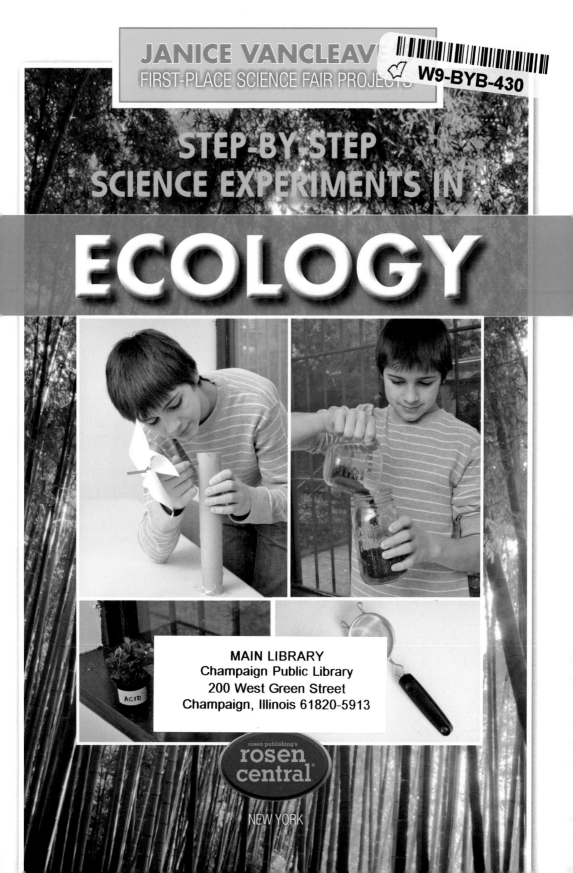

JANICE VANCLEAVE'S
FIRST-PLACE SCIENCE FAIR PROJECTS

STEP-BY-STEP
SCIENCE EXPERIMENTS IN

ECOLOGY

rosen publishing's
rosen
central

NEW YORK

This edition first published in 2013 by:

The Rosen Publishing Group, Inc.
29 East 21st Street
New York, NY 10010

Library of Congress Cataloging-in-Publication Data

VanCleave, Janice Pratt.
Step-by-step science experiments in ecology/Janice VanCleave.
    p. cm. — (Janice Vancleave's first-place science fair projects)
Includes bibliographical references and index.
ISBN 978-1-4488-6980-0 (library binding) —
ISBN 978-1-4488-8469-8 (pbk.) —
ISBN 978-1-4488-8470-4 (6-pack)
1. Ecology—Experiments—Juvenile literature. I. Title.
QH541.24.V36 2013
577—dc23

                                                                    2012007781

Manufactured in the United States of America

CPSIA Compliance Information: Batch #S12YA: For further information, contact Rosen Publishing, New York, New York, at 1-800-237-9932.

This edition published by arrangement with and permission of John Wiley & Sons, Inc., Hoboken, New Jersey.

Originally published as *Ecology For Every Kid.* Copyright © 1996 by John Wiley & Sons, Inc.

CONTENTS

INTRODUCTION

There was a time, many years ago, when observing nature was an activity best left to farmers and poets. To protect their livelihoods, the farmers needed to keep an eye on weather events and the cycle of the seasons, not to mention the nearby wildlife that might make a meal out of their livestock. Poets were concerned mainly with the beauty of the natural world. Then, in 1869, a German scientist named Ernst Haeckel gave a name to the watching of nature. The science of ecology was born.

Studying the interaction among living things and their environments is what ecology is all about. To do so requires a joining together of several branches of science. Biology, climatology, geology, and zoology all have their place in the study of ecology. Each branch offers vital information on one or more elements that coexist in various habitats.

Every inhabitant must be accounted for because each has a role to play. Life on Earth is a balancing act, one so delicate that any disruption to even the smallest living or nonliving element can have a ripple effect, upsetting the balance of nature in many areas. To prevent such problems, ecologists examine activity within the various types of life groups. Doing so allows them to figure out if everything is running smoothly and identify where trouble spots might occur.

How ecologists study the environment also requires close examination. For scientific purposes, the Earth is divided into several layers. The largest is the biosphere, which is the thin, life-supporting stratum of Earth's surface. The biosphere can be broken down into major life zones called biomes. But in order to fully understand how plants and creatures interact with one another, ecologists break things down even further. The majority of ecologists focus their studies on a smaller scale, at the population, community, and ecosystem levels.

As the size of the populations level off, ecologists study interactions within one particular species. They can gauge the balance of various populations by observing the size, density, and distribution of each. Communities provide details of how two or more species interact and what effect this has on the community as a whole. The examination of ecosystems shows how species of plants and animals interact with their physical surroundings. The flow of energy and nutrient cycling are the two most important factors at this level.

A lot has changed since Haeckel first coined the term "ecology." As threats such as pollution, species extinction, and global warming have cast their long shadows over the planet, the ecological sciences have grown in importance, becoming critical in international efforts to maintain and restore the environment to its most healthy state possible. Ecology will most likely be providing clues to the stability of the natural world for some time to come. After all, the life of every organism on Earth may very well hang in the balance.

Understanding basic ecology can help you think about how important you are and how you affect your natural surroundings. The decisions and changes you make can have a positive effect. If you know why plants and animals live in some places and not in others, you can help protect wildlife from waste or destruction.

How to Use This Book

Read each section slowly and follow all procedures carefully. You will learn best if each section is read in order, as there is some buildup of information as the book progresses. The format for each section is as follows:

- Purpose: A definition and explanation of facts you need to understand
- Materials: All the materials necessary for the experiment
- Procedure: a step-by-step explanation of the thought process
- Results: An explanation of the desired outcome of each experiment
- Why: A thorough explanation of the scientific reason for why the experiment produced its results

This book doesn't provide experiments for all the concepts you'll come across in your study of ecology, but it will offer basic examples of how nature works, enabling you to discover ways to be a part of making the world a better place to inhabit. It will guide you in understanding such concepts as how plant seeds spread, the food chain works, living things affect the ecosystem, the water cycle works, and the greenhouse effect works, among many others.

General Instructions for the Experiments

1. Read the experiment completely before starting.
2. Collect the appropriate supplies. You will have less frustration and more fun if all the materials necessary for the activity are ready before you start. You lose your train of thought when you have to stop and search for supplies.
3. Do not rush through the activity. Follow each step very carefully; never skip steps, and do not add your own. Safety is of the utmost importance, and by reading each activity before starting, then following the instructions exactly, you can feel confident that no unexpected results will occur.
4. Observe. If your results are not the same as those described in the activity, carefully reread the instructions and start over from step 1.

This book is designed to teach facts, concepts, and problem-solving strategies. The scientific concepts presented can be applied to many similar situations. The experiments were selected for their ability to be explained in basic terms with little complexity. One of the main objectives of the book is to present the fun of science.

SPREADER

PURPOSE: To determine how you affect the spreading of plant seeds in your environment.

MATERIALS:

- 8 tablespoons (120 ml) potting soil
- 4 5-ounce (150 ml) paper cups
- masking tape
- pencil
- small notebook
- shoe box
- rubber boots
- craft stick
- tap water

PROCEDURE:

NOTE: This experiment should be performed after it rains during the spring or summer.

1. Put a half-cup of potting soil in each of the four cups.
2. Use the tape and pencil to label the cups 1 through 4.

3. Place the cups, pencil, and notebook in the shoe box.

4. Put on your rubber boots.

5. Carrying the shoe box, take a walk through the woods or park, and walk across a muddy area on purpose.

6. Use the craft stick to scrape the mud from the bottom of your boots.

7. Add the mud to cup 1, and mix the mud and soil in the cup.

8. In the notebook, write a description of the area where the mud for cup 1 was collected.

9. Repeat steps 5 through 8 in a different muddy area for each of the other three cups, then go home.

10. With only the cups of soil and mud inside the shoe box, place the box where it will be warm and undisturbed, such as near a window.

11. Observe the contents of the cups each day for two weeks or until you observe plant growth. Water the soil in each cup once in a while to keep the soil moist (not wet).

RESULTS: Plants will usually be found growing in some and maybe all of the cups.

WHY?: The plants growing in the cups indicate that there were seeds present in the mud that stuck to your boots. Seeds from plants fall and become mixed in with the soil around them. As you walked through the mud, it stuck to the bottom of your boots. Some of the mud fell off your boots before you were able to scrape it into the cups. This fallen mud may have contained seeds. If the mud fell in an environment with the proper amount of warmth and moisture, the seeds would grow, just as the seeds in the cup grew.

MOVERS

PURPOSE: To determine an earthworm's niche.

MATERIALS:

- 2 cups (500 ml) dark-colored soil
- large bowl
- tap water
- spoon
- quart (liter) wide-mouthed jar
- 1 cup (250 ml) light-colored sand
- 1 tablespoon (15 ml) oats
- 10 to 12 earthworms (from a bait shop or dig your own)
- dark-colored construction paper
- rubber band

PROCEDURE:

1. Pour the soil into the bowl.
2. Slowly add water while stirring, until the soil is slightly moist.
3. Pour half of the moistened soil into the jar.
4. Pour the sand over the soil.
5. Add the remaining soil.

11

6. Sprinkle the oats over the soil.

7. Put the worms in the jar.

8. Wrap the paper around the jar and secure it with the rubber band. Place the jar in a cool place.

9. Every day for a week, remove the paper and observe the jar for a few minutes. Then, put the paper back over the jar and put the jar away.

10. At the end of the week, release the worms where you found them or in any outdoor garden or wooded area.

RESULTS The worms start wiggling and burrow into the soil. After a few days, tunnels can be seen in the soil, and the dark soil and light sand become mixed.

WHY? An earthworm's niche is very simple compared to the niches of many other organisms. The worm lives in and eats its way through the soil. It gets nourishment from the remains of other living things, especially plants, contained in the soil. The worm's movements loosen the soil so that water and air needed by plants can more easily pass through it. The worm's waste also adds to the soil nutrients that the plants need.

SMALL PORTION

PURPOSE: To demonstrate the amount of land available for agriculture.

MATERIALS:

- red, blue, yellow, and green modeling clay
- knife (to be used only by an adult)
- adult helper

PROCEDURE:

1. Shape a piece of the red clay into a ball about the size of an apple.

2. Ask an adult to cut a ¼ section from the ball.

2

3. Cover the curved surface of the ¾ section with blue clay. Cover the curved surface of the ¼ section with yellow clay.

4. Ask an adult to help cut the ¼ section in half lengthwise to make two ⅛ sections.

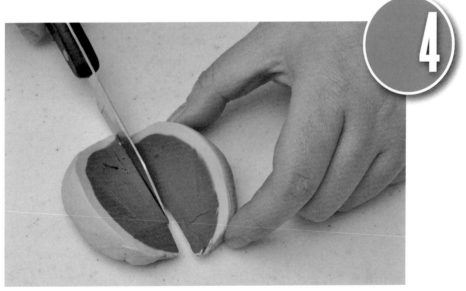

5. Ask an adult to cut one of the ⅛ sections into four equal parts to make four ¹⁄₃₂ sections.

6. Cover the curved surface of one of the $\frac{1}{32}$ sections with green clay.

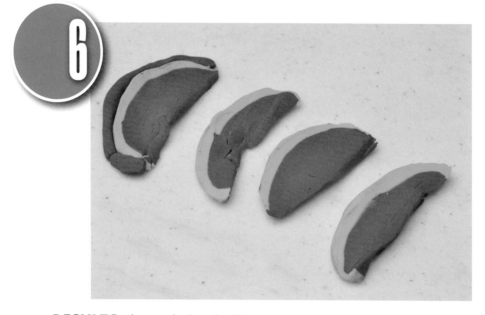

RESULTS The red clay ball is cut into six separate pieces and the curved surfaces are covered with different colors of clay. One curved surface is blue, four are yellow, and one is green. All the flat surfaces remain red.

WHY? The red ball represents the Earth. The ¾ section covered in blue represents the area of the Earth covered by oceans. The yellow $\frac{1}{8}$ section represents land areas such as the Antarctic, deserts, mountains, and swamps, where no crops can be grown. The three yellow $\frac{1}{32}$ sections represent land areas that are too wet, too hot, or too rocky, or that have soil that is too poor for agriculture. The last $\frac{1}{32}$ section, covered in green, represents the land area where all food and other agricultural products are produced.

PARTNERS

PURPOSE: To examine a lichen.

MATERIALS:

- 2 or 3 samples of lichen (a pale green scaly or leafy patch generally found on the north side of trees)
- desk lamp
- magnifying lens
- small bowl
- small drinking glass
- tap water
- eyedropper

PROCEDURE

1. Hold one of the lichen samples under the desk lamp.

2. Use the magnifying lens to study the entire outer surface of the lichen.

3. Place another lichen sample in the bowl.

4. Fill the glass half full with water.

5. Use the eyedropper to add two to three drops of water to the surface of the lichen in the bowl.

RESULTS The surface of the lichen has green and white areas. The lichen absorbs the water like a sponge.

WHY? Lichen is a combination of green algae and a colorless fungus. Lichen is an example of mutualism. The green algae contains chlorophyll, a green light-absorbing pigment used in photosynthesis. Photosynthesis is the process by which plants use light energy trapped by chlorophyll to change a gas in the air, called carbon dioxide, and water into food for the plant. The algae's food is shared with the fungus, which has no chlorophyll and therefore cannot make its own food. Instead, the fungus absorbs water which contains minerals vital for it and the algae's survival. The fungus has tiny strands by which it attaches to sur-faces, such as tree bark, to anchor the lichen. Both organisms benefit from their relationship.

AROUND AND AROUND

PURPOSE: To construct a model of a food chain.

MATERIALS:

- drawing compass
- typing paper
- scissors
- pencil
- 18-by-8-inch (45-by-20-cm) piece of dark-colored poster board (such as red or blue)
- ruler
- paper brad
- transparent tape
- adult helper

PROCEDURE:

1. Use the compass to draw a 7-inch (17.5-cm) -diameter circle on the paper.

2

2. Cut out the circle.

3. Divide the circle into three equal parts, and add the animals, plants, bacteria, and labels that are in a food chain in order. This circle will be called the food chain wheel.

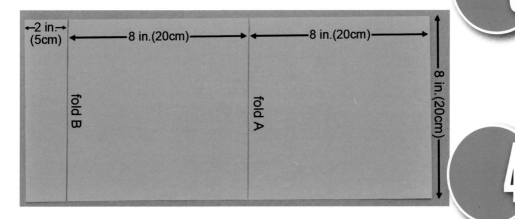

4. On the poster board, measure and mark the fold lines as shown.

5. Fold the poster board along fold line A. The longer side of the poster board will be called the front side.

6. On the front side of the poster board, mark a dot 6 inches (15 cm) from one short edge and 4 inches (10 cm) from each long edge, as shown.

7. Draw a triangle along the fold, beginning 1 inch (2.5 cm) from each long edge and up to a point ¼ inch (0.6 cm) from the center dot.

8. Cut out the triangle through both thicknesses of poster board.

9. Have an adult use the compass to punch a hole in the center of the food chain wheel and through the center dot on the poster board. Be sure to punch the hole through both thicknesses of the poster board.

10. Insert the food chain wheel between the two thicknesses of the poster board so that the drawing faces the front side of the poster board.

11. Insert the brad through the holes in all three layers, and secure it to the back side of the poster board.

12. Fold the poster board along fold line B and secure with tape.

13. Hold the poster board with the front side facing you.

14. Turn the food chain wheel in a counterclockwise direction.

15. Observe the sequence of pictures in the triangular window.

RESULTS A model showing the transfer of energy in a food chain is made.

WHY? One part of the food chain at a time is seen in the window. As the wheel turns, the next level in the food chain is revealed. You can follow the transfer of energy from producer to consumer to decomposer and then back again to producer.

SOAKER

PURPOSE: To show how weeds help moisten soil.

MATERIALS:

- ruler
- masking tape
- two 7-oz. (210-ml) plastic drinking cups
- marking pen
- potting soil
- 3 craft sticks
- tap water
- timer

PROCEDURE:

1. Place a 2-inch (5-cm) piece of tape on the side of each cup so that one end of the tape touches the rim of the cup.

2. Make a mark on the tape ½ inch (1.25 cm) from the top of the cup.

3. Pack soil into the cups up to the bottom edge of the tape.

4. Move each craft stick back and forth slightly as you insert the three sticks into the soil of one cup.

5. Add water up to the mark in each cup, and then mark the height again after one minute.

RESULTS The height of the water in the cup with the sticks is lower than that in the cup without the sticks.

WHY? When water is added to the cup with the sticks, the water runs into the openings the sticks make in the soil. The growing roots of weeds, or the roots of all plants, like inserting the sticks, make tiny openings as they move through the soil. This allows rainwater to fill the openings and soak into the soil instead of running over its surface. Water that soaks into the soil can be used by weeds and other plants.

HOME ALONE

PURPOSE: To demonstrate how plants can live without animals.

MATERIALS:
- 1 cup (250 ml) potting soil
- quart (liter) jar, with lid
- clump of grass
- tap water

PROCEDURE:

1. Pour the soil into the jar.

2. Insert a clump of grass that will fit inside the jar.

3. Moisten the soil with water so that it is damp but not too wet.

4. Secure the lid on the jar.

5. Place the jar near a window but not in direct sunlight.

6. Observe the jar during the daytime and nighttime as often as possible for two weeks.

RESULTS The inside of the jar appears cloudy at times during the daytime. Water droplets appear on the inside of the glass during the nighttime and parts of the day.

WHY? The grass survives in the jar because plants make many of the materials that they need for survival. Plants can live without animals, but animals cannot live without plants because animals cannot make oxygen or produce their own food. If all the plants on the Earth were destroyed, oxygen would be used up and the animals would die unless a way was found to replace the oxygen and food produced by plants.

DRIPPER

PURPOSE: To demonstrate the water cycle.

MATERIALS:

- tap water
- ruler
- transparent storage box about the size of a shoe box
- plastic wrap
- ice cube
- resealable plastic bag
- timer

PROCEDURE:

1. Pour 1 inch (2.5 cm) of water into the box.

2. Cover the top of the box with plastic wrap.

3. Put the ice cube in the bag and seal the bag.

4. Place the bag in the center of the plastic wrap that covers the box.

5. Gently push the ice down about 1 inch (2.5 cm) so that the plastic wrap slopes down toward the center.

6. Set the box near a window so that the sunlight shines on the box.

7. Observe the surface of the plastic directly under the ice cube every twenty minutes for one hour or until the ice melts.

RESULTS Water droplets form on the underside of the plastic under the ice. Some of these water droplets fall back into the water in the box.

WHY? The heat from the sun provides energy, causing some of the liquid water in the box to evaporate. The water vapor rises and condenses on the underside of the plastic, which has been cooled by the ice. As more water collects on the plastic, the droplets increase in size until their weight causes them to fall back into the water below. This is a model of the water cycle on the Earth. The bottom of the box represents the surface of the Earth, and the plastic represents the Earth's atmosphere. As long as the box remains closed, the amount of water in the box remains the same; it just changes from one form to another.

DIGGER

PURPOSE: To simulate a woodpecker's special adaptation for obtaining food.

MATERIALS:

- raisin cookie
- paper plate
- pen
- round toothpick

PROCEDURE:

CAUTION: Do not eat the food materials in this experiment.

1. Place the cookie on the plate.

2. Use the pointed end of the pen to dig out the parts of the cookie from around one of the raisins.

3. Use the toothpick to spear the raisin and remove it from the cookie.

RESULTS The pen's point breaks away pieces of the cookie from around the raisin. The toothpick easily sticks into the raisin, allowing you to remove it from the cookie.

WHY? The pen represents the strong chisel-like bill of the wood-pecker, which is used to dig insects out of wood. The toothpick represents the woodpecker's lancelike tongue, which is used to spear the exposed insects.

The bill and tongue of the woodpecker are special physical adaptations of this bird. Birds that live in different environments have their own special physical adaptations for securing food. For example, the pelican has a large dipper-shaped bill to scoop fish from the water. The pelican cannot dig insects out of trees, and the woodpecker cannot scoop fish from the water. Each is adapted to its own environment.

BRRR

PURPOSE: To determine how skin covering protects animals from the cold.

MATERIALS:
- 5 to 6 ice cubes
- large bowl
- tap water
- thermometer
- timer
- paper towel
- wool glove
- plastic bag

PROCEDURE:
1. Place the ice cubes in the bowl and fill the bowl with water.
2. Allow the thermometer to sit for ten minutes so that it records the correct temperature of the air in the room.
3. Hold the thermometer in your hand and place your thumb over the bulb.
4. Gently press your thumb against the bulb for five seconds.
   CAUTION: Do not press too hard. The glass bulb could break.

5. Observe the change in the temperature reading as you hold the bulb.

6. Place the same hand in the bowl of ice water for five seconds.

7. Dry your hand with the paper towel. Immediately hold the thermometer in your chilled hand and press your thumb against the bulb for five seconds.

8. Observe the change in the temperature reading.

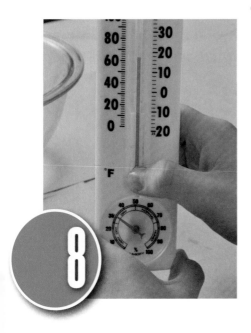

9. Repeat steps 3 through 6, wearing the wool glove. Place your gloved hand inside the plastic bag for step 6 to keep the glove from getting wet.

10. Remove the bag and glove from your hand. Immediately hold the thermometer in your chilled hand and press your thumb against the bulb for five seconds.

RESULTS Holding the thermometer with your hand at normal body temperature causes the reading to increase. The thermometer reading decreases when the bulb is pressed by your chilled hand. The chilled gloved hand stays warmer than the chilled hand without the glove.

WHY? Heat energy moves from warmer objects to cooler objects. A thermometer indicates whether an object is giving out heat or taking in heat. At the beginning of the experiment, your thumb is at its normal body temperature of about 98.6° Fahrenheit (37° Celsius). Body temperature is usually greater than room temperature, so the thermometer reading should increase when you hold your warm hand against the bulb. The second, lower reading indicates that, after being placed in ice water, your skin has lost heat energy and is cooler than normal body temperature. The wool glove acts as an insulator (a material that does not easily gain or lose energy) in that it keeps the heat of your hand from being lost to the cold water. The insulating glove keeps your hand warmer, just as insulating fur and feathers on animals keep their skin warmer.

NIBBLERS

PURPOSE: To determine why grass can survive being nibbled by animals.

MATERIALS:

- potting soil
- trowel
- clump of grass
- pencil
- construction paper
- tap water
- ruler
- marking pen

PROCEDURE:

1. Put the soil in the cup.

2. With permission, use the trowel to dig up a clump of grass that will fit in the paper cup. Choose a clump that has at least three stems, and make sure you dig up as many of the grass roots as possible.

3. Plant the grass in the soil.

4. Use the pencil to punch three or four holes on the side of the cup around the bottom edge.

5. Set the cup in a saucer.

6. Moisten the soil with water and keep the soil moist, but not wet, during the experiment.

7. Locate the nodes (where leaves grow from a stem) on each grass stem.

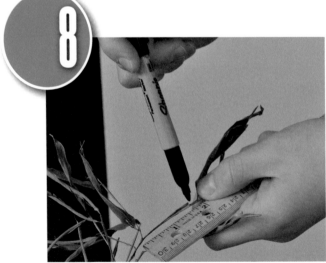

8. Use the ruler and pen to mark three equal sections on one of the stems between two nodes at the top of the stem.

9. Repeat step 8 for the other two stems, marking the second and third highest pair of nodes, respectively.
10. Set the plant in an area where it will receive sunlight all or most of the day.
11. At the end of seven days, measure the distance between the marks on the stems.

RESULTS The distance between the lower node and the first mark above this node increases the most on all the stems. Any increase in distance between the remaining marks is slight to none as the marks approach the higher node.

WHY? Grasses grow above each node along the stem, not from the tips as other plants do. Even with the loss of large portions of stem, lower areas continue to grow. This type of growth allows grass to survive nibbling by animals.

12 EXPANDABLE SKIN

PURPOSE: To demonstrate how some cactus plants store water.

MATERIALS:

- typing paper
- 1-gallon (4-liter) plastic food bag (such as a produce bag)
- tape

PROCEDURE:

1. Fold the paper like a fan, beginning at one short end. Each fold should be about ½ inch (1.3 cm) wide.

2. Fold the plastic bag in thirds.

3. Lay the folded bag on top of the folded paper with the bottom of the bag even with the edge of the paper. Tape the bottom of the bag to the edge of the paper.

4. Wrap the paper so that it forms a cylinder around the bag. Secure the ends of the paper with tape.

5. Stand the paper cylinder on a table with the open end of the plastic bag up.

6. Observe the size of the paper cylinder.

7. Open the top of the bag. Blow into the bag while holding it with your hand.

8. Keep the air inside the bag by squeezing the top closed with your hand.

9. Again, observe the size of the paper cylinder.

10. Release the bag, then use your hands to gently squeeze the paper pleats back into place.

11. Again observe the size of the cylinder.

RESULTS The cylinder enlarges when the bag inside is filled with air. Squeezing the cylinder returns it to its smaller folded shape.

WHY? Adding air to the bag causes it to enlarge. As the bag enlarges, it pushes outward on the paper cylinder. This outward pressure causes the pleats in the paper to unfold and the cylinder to increase in size. As the pleats unfold, the shape of the cylinder changes as the surface becomes smoother.

This experiment demonstrates the way some cacti, such as the saguaro, hold extra water. Saguaros grow very high and have trunks that are pleated like the paper. A 20-foot (6-m) plant may store more than 100 gallons (380 liters) of water. This water pushes outward, causing the saguaro's pleated surface to unfold. Cacti may increase in size as much as 20 percent during the rainy season. During times without rain, cacti use their stored water and shrink back to a smaller size and shape.

SHOCK ABSORBERS

PURPOSE: To determine why mountain goats are able to move around surefootedly on rocky slopes.

MATERIALS:

- child's sock
- 1 cup (250 ml) uncooked rice
- 9-ounce (270-ml) plastic drinking cup with a flat bottom
- white paper
- marking pen

PROCEDURE:

1. Fill the sock with rice.
2. Tie a knot in the top of the sock.
3. Place the sock in the cup.

4. Set the cup in the center of the paper on a level surface, such as a tabletop. With the pen, trace the outline of the bottom of the cup on the paper.

5. Raise the cup above the circle drawn on the paper. Make an effort to position the cup above the paper so that it will fall straight down and land in the circle when dropped.

6. Drop the cup.

7. Observe where the cup lands, and note any movement it makes after landing.

8. Repeat steps 5 to 7 four times.

9. Remove the sock from the cup.

10. Hold the sock about the same height as before above the circle. Make an effort to position the sock so that it will fall straight down and land in the circle when dropped.

12

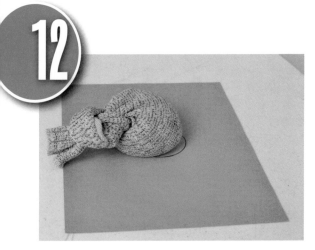

11. Drop the sock.
12. Observe where the sock lands, and note any movement it makes after landing.
13. Repeat steps 10 to 12 four times.

RESULTS When the sock is in the cup, it lands in the circle, but the cup usually bounces upon landing and either falls over or moves partly out of the circle. The sock alone lands in the circle each time and does not bounce.

WHY? Newton's third law of motion states that for every action there is an equal but opposite reaction. This means that the paper and tabletop push up on the cup and sock with the same force that the cup and sock push down on the paper and tabletop. This upward push causes the cup to bounce. The tabletop and paper also push up on the sock alone, but the sock does not bounce because, unlike the cup, its surface is soft and flexible.

Flexibility allows parts of the sock to move up and down without moving the entire sock. This independent movement allows the sock to absorb the shock of landing and not bounce around. The soft pads in the center of the hard hooves of a goat, like the sock, also act as shock absorbers. When a goat walks or leaps from one rock to the next, any bounce is absorbed by the soft, flexible footpads.

UNDERWATER FOREST

PURPOSE: To build a model of kelp.

MATERIALS:

- scissors
- empty 2-quart (2-liter) plastic soda bottle
- ruler
- aluminum foil
- pipe cleaner
- 2 round plastic fishing corks, 1 inch (2.5 cm) in diameter, with spring-type clips
- rock
- tap water
- adult helper

PROCEDURE:

1. Ask an adult to cut the top off the soda bottle to make an open container about 8 inches (20 cm) tall.

2. Cut an 8-by-6-inch (20-by-15-cm) strip of foil.

3. Fold the foil strip in half lengthwise four times.

4. Wrap about 2 inches (5 cm) of one end of the foil strip around the center of the pipe cleaner.

5. Clip the bottom of one cork to the foil strip 2 inches (5 cm) above the pipe cleaner.

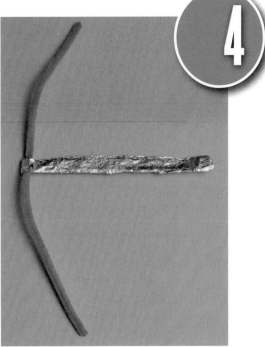

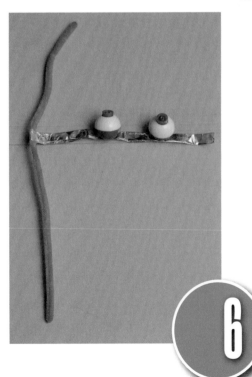

6. Clip the bottom of the second cork 2 inches (5 cm) above the first cork.

7. Cut two long triangles from the aluminum foil, each with a base of 1 inch (2.5 cm) and sides of 6 inches (15 cm).

11

8. Clip the top of each cork to the base of one of the foil triangles.
9. Wrap the pipe cleaner around the rock.
10. Fill about three-quarters of the soda bottle with water.
11. Carefully lower the rock and attachments into the water.

RESULTS The corks float at different depths along with the attached foil triangles.

WHY? Underwater forests of tall, brown algae (simple plantlike organisms found in water or on wet surfaces), called kelp, grow in cool coastal waters. These thick strands of kelp provide living spaces for hundreds of different kinds of ocean organisms. Kelp varies in height from 1.5 feet (4.5 m) to 198 feet (60 m).

Most kelps consist of at least four distinguishable parts: the holdfast (represented by pipe cleaner), the stipe (foil strip), the float (cork), and the blade (foil triangle). The holdfast is a root-like structure that clings to rocks and other hard surfaces on the ocean floor, keeping the kelp from floating to the surface. The stipe is a stemlike structure to which the blades are attached.

The float is an air-filled structure at the base of each blade that lifts the kelp so that it stands upright. The blade is a leaflike structure where photosynthesis occurs.

POLLUTION DILUTION

PURPOSE: To show how adding substances to water affects pollution.

MATERIALS:
- cup
- quart (liter) jar
- gallon (4-liter) jug, with lid
- tap water
- red food coloring
- spoon
- adult helper

PROCEDURE:

1. Fill the cup, jar, and jug three-fourths full with water.
2. Add and stir in two drops of food coloring to the water in the cup.

2

3

3. Pour all but a small amount of the water from the cup into the jar and stir.

49

4. Pour all but a small amount of the water from the jar into the jug.

5. Place the lid on the jug and shake the jug back and forth to mix thoroughly.

6. Compare the color of the water left in the cup and jar with the color of the water in the jug.

RESULTS The water is dark red in the cup, pale red in the jar, and pale pink to colorless in the jug.

WHY? The red color is most intense in the cup because the molecules (the smallest parts of a substance that have all the characteristics of the substance) of red coloring are close together and reflect more red light to your eyes. When this colored water is added to clean water, the color molecules spread evenly throughout the water. By the time the color molecules are added to the clean water in the jug, they are far enough apart to become very pale to invisible because of their small size.

This is what happens with some water pollutants. The material may be visible where it is initially dumped into a river, but as it flows downstream and becomes mixed with more water, it can no longer be seen with the naked eye. This does not mean that the pollutant is gone. Animal and plant life in a stream is affected by pollutants many miles from the source. The degree of harm to the animal depends on the type of pollutant and how much water has been added in order to dilute (lessen the strength by mixing with another material, usually water) the pollutant.

16 BOUNCE BACK

PURPOSE: To simulate the greenhouse effect.

MATERIALS:

- 2 cups (500 ml) soil
- 1 lidded jar (tall enough to hold one of the thermometers)
- 2 thermometers

PROCEDURE:

1. Put the soil in the jar.
2. Place one of the thermometers inside the jar and secure the lid.

3. Place the jar near a window in direct sunlight, and place the second thermometer next to the jar.

4. Observe the temperature readings on both thermom-eters after thirty minutes.

RESULTS The temperature reading inside the closed jar is higher than that outside the jar.

WHY? The jar is a small model of a greenhouse. A green-house is made of glass or clear plastic, which allows solar energy to pass through and heat the contents.

Like a greenhouse, solar energy enters and warms the Earth's atmosphere. A greenhouse warms mainly because it is closed and the cooler air outside is prevented from mixing with the warm air inside. The Earth warms because solar energy strikes the Earth's surface and the surface gives off heat. Most of this heat is absorbed by the greenhouse gases, trapping the heat close to the earth.

EXPERIMENT 17

FOAMY

PURPOSE: To make simulated plastic foam.

MATERIALS:

- 1 cup (250 ml) cold tap water
- 2-quart (2-liter) bowl
- 2 tablespoons (30 ml) dishwashing liquid
- whisk

- mixing spoon
- 1-cup (250-ml) measuring cup
- timer
- 1-tablespoon (15-ml) measuring spoon

PROCEDURE:

1. Pour the water into the bowl.

2. Add the dishwashing liquid to the water in the bowl.

2

3. Use the whisk to beat the liquid until you have made a big mound of foam.

4. Use the mixing spoon to fill the measuring cup with foam. *NOTE:* Be careful not to transfer any liquid to the cup.

5. Put the cup where it will not be disturbed.

6. Observe the foam as often as possible for four hours.

7. After four hours, or when all the foam has changed to a liquid, use the measuring spoon to measure the liquid in the cup.

RESULTS When foamy, the bubbles fill the cup. After the bubbles have popped, the cupful of foam changes to about 2 tablespoons (30 ml) of liquid.

WHY? Beating the liquid produces bubbles filled with air. The foam is mostly air. When the cup is allowed to sit, the bubbles break, the air escapes, and the foam turns back to a soapy liquid. Like the soap foam, plastic foam is full of air. But unlike the soap foam, the bubbles don't break unless pressure is applied, so plastic foam stays the same size. Because plastic foam is mostly air, large materials made with this plastic are very lightweight and easy to transport. Air does not transmit energy easily, so air-filled plastic is a good insulator, which is good. However, such plastics take up large amounts of space in garbage dumps, which is bad.

MISTY

PURPOSE: To demonstrate the effect of acid rain on plants.

MATERIALS:

- 2 quart (liter) spray bottles
- distilled water
- masking tape
- marking pen
- white vinegar
- 3 small house plants that are as similar as possible

PROCEDURE:

1. Fill one spray bottle with distilled water. Secure the lid.

2. Use the tape and pen to label the bottle "Water." This solution will be referred to as the water.

3

3. Fill the second spray bottle half full with distilled water, then add enough vinegar to fill the bottle.
4. Secure the lid and shake the bottle back and forth several times to mix its contents.
5. Label the second bottle "Acid." This solution will be referred to as the acid.

6. Label the plants "Acid," "Dry," and "Water." In the remaining steps, treat each plant exactly the same except for watering.
7. Spray the water on the soil of the plant labeled "Water" until it is damp but not wet. Count the number of squirts of water added to the plant.
8. Spray an equal amount of the acid on the soil of the plant labeled "Acid."
9. Do not water the plant labeled "Dry."
10. Place all three plants near a window so that they receive equal amounts of sunlight.

10

11. Once a day, spray the leaves of the plants labeled "Water" and "Acid" with three squirts of the appropriate solution.
12. Spray equal amounts of solution on the soil of the plants labeled "Water" and "Acid" as needed to keep the soil moist.
13. Do not water the plant labeled "Dry."
14. Observe the plants for four weeks or until one plant loses at least half its leaves or dies.

RESULTS The dry plant dies. Its leaves become pale and eventually fall off. The leaves of the plant sprayed with acid become pale and some turn yellow before falling. This plant also dies. The amount of time for these results varies with the type of plant used. The plant sprayed with water remains healthy.

NOTE These are the expected results, but an unhealthy plant could die even if sprayed with water.

WHY? Distilled water has a pH of 7. It is neutral—neither acidic nor basic. You can see that water is necessary for the survival of plants, because the dry plant dies without it. While plants remain healthy in slightly acidic rainfall, they cannot survive in low pH—high acid levels. The acid level of the vinegar solution is higher than most acid rain and higher than most common plants can endure, but some plants are more tolerant of acid and will survive for a longer period of time.

SUNBLOCK

PURPOSE: To simulate the effect of the ozone layer on light.

MATERIALS:

- clear plastic report folder
- sunblock lotion with high SPF rating
- sheet of newspaper
- masking tape
- modeling clay
- timer

PROCEDURE:

NOTE: The experiment works best if started at noon on a sunny day.

1. Use your fingers to coat one side of the folder with the lotion, making sure to apply it in an even layer. Wash your hands after applying the lotion.

1

2. Place the news-
paper on a
table outdoors.

3. Secure the
paper by taping
the corners to
the table.

4. Use as many walnut-size balls of clay as needed to
support the folder lotion side up over the center of the
newspaper. Support the center of the folder with clay if
necessary to keep it from touching the paper.

NOTE: You only want to test the effects of reduction of UV light, not the reduction of air. The folder is raised so that air can flow over the paper.

5. After two hours, remove the folder and compare the color of the newspaper under the area where the folder was placed with the color of the area outside the folder.

RESULTS The area of the newspaper covered by the folder remained white, while the area outside the plastic turned yellow.

WHY? The paper used to make newspaper has a yellow color before it is whitened by removing oxygen. Newspapers yellow with age, because over a period of time oxygen in the air gets added back into the paper. UV light from the sun speeds up the rate at which oxygen combines with the paper, thus reducing the time needed to yellow the paper. The sunblock lotion, like the ozone layer, prevented most of the UV light from hitting the paper.

FILL 'ER UP

PURPOSE: To see how different materials change in a landfill.

MATERIALS:

- scissors
- ruler
- plastic trash bag
- 2 shoe boxes
- masking tape
- enough soil to fill both shoe boxes
- large bowl
- tap water
- 2 sets of test materials: newspaper, orange peel, aluminum foil, plastic lid
- magnifying lens

PROCEDURE:

1. Cut two 22-by-22-inch (55-by-55-cm) pieces from the trash bag.

2. Line each shoe box with one piece of plastic.

3. Secure the plastic lining with tape.

63

5

4. Place the soil in the bowl and add enough water to moisten it.

5. Place about 2 inches (5 cm) of moistened soil in each box.

6. On the surface of the soil in each box, place one of each test material. Spread the materials so that they do not touch each other.

6

7

7. Fill each box with soil to cover the test materials.

8. Place the boxes in a sunny place. For the next twenty-eight days, keep the soil in each box moist by adding equal amounts of water to each. Treat the boxes exactly the same.
9. After the first fourteen days, carefully uncover the test materials of one box.
10. Use the magnifying lens to study the materials.
11. After fourteen more days, uncover the materials of the second box.
12. Again, study the materials with the magnifying lens.

RESULTS After fourteen days, the aluminum foil and plastic lid remain unchanged. The newspaper and orange peel show some signs of breaking down. After twenty-eight days, the aluminum foil and plastic lid still remain unchanged, and the newspaper and orange peel show more signs of breaking down.

WHY? When garbage is thrown into a landfill, it is hoped that microorganisms (microscopic living organisms) in the soil will cause the materials to decompose. Some materials take longer than others to decompose. Things like paper and food substances can take only a few days, while plastics and aluminum cans are predicted to take hundreds of years, if they decompose at all.

21 WIND POWER

PURPOSE: To show how wind can be used to perform work.

MATERIALS:

- scissors
- ruler
- typing paper
- thick pencil
- coin
- paper hole-punch
- drinking straw

- modeling clay
- cardboard tube from a roll of paper towels
- masking tape
- thread
- paper clip
- fan

PROCEDURE:

1. Cut a 6-by-6-inch (15-by-15-cm) square from the paper.

2. Draw two diagonal lines across the paper square so that you have an X.

3. Use the coin to draw a circle in the center of the paper.

2

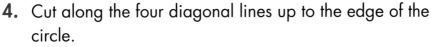

4. Cut along the four diagonal lines up to the edge of the circle.

5. With the hole-punch, make a hole in the center of the circle and at each corner as shown.

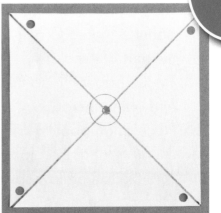

6. Fold each corner so its hole aligns over the center hole. The folded corners will be called blades.

7. Push the drinking straw through all the holes, and position the blades near one end of the straw so that the folded corners face away from the straw.

8. Wrap a small piece of clay around both sides of the straw next to the blades to keep them in place.

9. With the hole-punch, make two holes opposite each other near one end of the cardboard tube.

10. Insert the pencil in the holes in the tube and move the pencil around to make the holes slightly larger than the straw.

11. Tape the other end of the tube near the edge of a table.

12. Insert the free end of the straw through the holes in the tube so that the blades face the center of the table.

13. Cut a 2-foot (60-cm) piece of thread.
14. Tape one end of the thread about 2 inches (5 cm) from the end of the straw.
15. Tie the paper clip to the free end of the thread.
16. Place a fan about 1 foot (30 cm) in front of the blades.
17. Turn the fan on low speed.
18. Observe the movement of the blades, straw, and paper clip.

RESULTS The blades and the straw turn. The string winds around the turning straw, lifting the paper clip.

WHY? The paper blades are a model of a simple machine called a wheel and axle. This machine, which consists of a large wheel to which a smaller wheel or axle is attached, is used to lift objects. The model demonstrates how a windmill works.

The wind from the fan hits against the model windmill's blades (the wheel), turning them around. The wheel turns in a large circle, making the straw (the axle) turn in a smaller circle. As the wheel makes one large turn, the string winds once around the turning axle. The model windmill, like real windmills, harnesses the energy of wind to perform work. Windmills can be used to pump water, grind grain, or produce electricity.

TOO MUCH, TOO FAST

PURPOSE: To demonstrate the effect of overfishing.

MATERIALS:

- scissors
- 2 dishwashing sponges
- large bowl
- tap water
- small tea strainer
- small bowl
- large tea strainer
- helper

PROCEDURE:

1. Cut each sponge into 1-inch (2.5-cm) cubes.

2. Fill the large bowl with water.

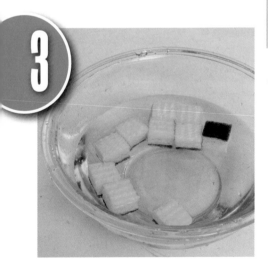

3. Place ten sponge cubes in the water, spreading the cubes over the water's surface.

69

4. Ask your helper to close his or her eyes and move the small strainer through the water once to scoop up as many cubes as possible.

5. Remove the cubes from the strainer and place them in the small bowl.

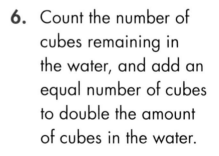

6. Count the number of cubes remaining in the water, and add an equal number of cubes to double the amount of cubes in the water.

7. Repeat steps 4 to 6 three times. On the last scooping, do not add any cubes.
8. Start over with ten cubes in the water.
9. Ask your helper to do steps 4 and 5 four times using the large strainer. After the last time, count the cubes remaining in the water and add an equal number of cubes to double the amount of cubes in the water.

RESULTS The number of cubes in the bowl increases when the small strainer was used and cubes were added after each scooping. The number of cubes greatly decreases and may even be zero after four scoops with the large strainer.

WHY? The sponge cubes represent fish and the strainers commercial fishing nets. Scooping with the small strainer is like fishing with fewer nets and catching fewer fish. Adding cubes represents reproduction of fish. With a need to provide fish to feed the growing human population, commercial fishing boats haul in more fish. Large catches are a problem when the fish that are left cannot lay their eggs fast enough to keep up. Overfishing removes fish faster than they can reproduce as demonstrated by using the large strainer and not adding cubes after each scooping. Some fish are in danger of becoming extinct because of overfishing.

GLOSSARY

acid A solution that has a pH less than 7; also a solution having this pH value.

algae Simple plantlike organisms found in water or on wet surfaces.

atmosphere The layer of air surrounding the Earth.

carbon dioxide A gas found in air that is used in photosynthesis and produced by respiration; one of the greenhouse gases.

chlorophyll A green light-absorbing pigment used in photosynthesis.

colony A large population whose members depend on each other.

condensation The process by which a gas, such as water vapor, changes to a liquid when cooled; also the water that results from this process.

condense To change from a gas to a liquid as a result of being cooled.

consumers Organisms (specifically, animals) that are not able to produce their own food and must eat other organisms.

decomposers Organisms such as bacteria and fungi that decompose dead plants and animals.

dilute To lessen the strength of a material by mixing it with another material, usually water.

disperse To spread to another location.

ecological community The interaction of living organisms with their environment.

ecosystem A distinct area that combines biotic communities and the abiotic environments with which they interact.

evaporate To change from a liquid to a gas as a result of being heated.

fertilize To join male sperm with a female egg.

greenhouse gases Atmospheric gases, mostly carbon dioxide and water vapor, that trap the warmth from the sun, just as glass traps warmth in a greenhouse.

insulator A material that does not easily gain or lose energy.

kelp Underwater forests of tall, brown algae that grow in cool coastal waters.

lichen A combination of two organisms, fungus and green algae, that live in a relationship of mutualism.

microorganisms Living organisms so small they can only be seen through a microscope.

molecule The smallest part of a substance that has all the characteristics of the substance.

node Where leaves grow from a plant stem.

pH The unit of measure for determining whether a solution is acidic, basic, or neutral.

photosynthesis The process by which plants use light energy trapped by chlorophyll to change carbon dioxide and water into food.

tropical rain forest A forest that gains more water from precipitation than it loses through evaporation. These forests are located in the tropical zone and having an average temperature between 70° and 85°F (21° and 29°C) and average yearly rainfall of more than 80 inches (200 cm).

Environment Canada
Inquiry Centre
70 Crémazie Street
Gatineau, QC K1A 0H3
Canada
(800) 668-6767 (in Canada only)
(819) 997-2800
Web site: http://www.ec.gc.ca
Environment Canada's mission is to preserve and enhance
   the quality of Canada's natural environment.

GrassRoots Recycling Network
P.O. Box 282
Cotati, CA 94931
(707) 321-7883
Web site: http://www.grrn.org
This network of activists and recycling professionals is dedicated
   to the idea of Zero Waste—not wasting any resources.

National Ecological Observatory Network (NEON)
1685 38th Street, Suite 100
Boulder, CO 80301
(720) 746-4844
Website: www.neoninc.org
Funded by the National Science Fund, NEON is a national
   network of ecological observation sites. The organization
   collects data from across the United States on the impact
   of climate change, land use change, and invasive species

on natural resources and biodiversity. NEON is developing workshops, internships, and research opportunities in ecology.

National Forest Protection Alliance
P.O. Box 8264
Missoula, MT 59807
(406) 542-7565
Web site: http://www.forestadvocate.org
The National Forest Protection Alliance is a network of organizations that takes action to protect and restore America's national forests.

The Nature Conservancy
4245 North Fairfax Drive, Suite 100
Arlington, VA 22203-1606
(703) 841-5300
Web site: http://www.nature.org
Founded in 1951, the Nature Conservancy works around the world to protect ecologically important lands and waters for nature and people.

Recycling Council of Ontario
215 Spadina Avenue, #407
Toronto, ON M5T 2C7
Canada
(416) 657-2797
Web site: http://www.rco.on.ca

This nonprofit agency in Canada teaches people how to reduce waste and how to get rid of waste in a more environmentally friendly way.

U.S. Environmental Protection Agency
Ariel Rios Building
1200 Pennsylvania Avenue NW
Washington, DC 20460
(202) 272-0167
Web site: http://www.epa.gov
The U.S. Environmental Protection Agency was established in 1970 to protect people's health and the environment. The agency conducts research on environmental issues, develops and enforces regulations, and provides funding for research by universities and nonprofit organizations.

Web Sites

Due to the changing nature of Internet links, Rosen Publishing has developed an online list of Web sites related to the subject of this book. This site is updated regularly. Please use this link to access the list:

http://www.rosenlinks.com/scif/eco

FOR FURTHER READING

Adair, Rick. *Critical Perspectives on Politics and the Environment* (Scientific American Critical Anthologies on Environment and Climate). New York, NY: Rosen Publishing, 2006.

Adams, Simon, Anita Ganeri, and Ann Kay. *Geography of the World*. London, England: DK, 2006.

Barraclough, Sue. *Recycling Materials* (Making a Difference). Mankato, MN: Sea to Sea Publications, 2007.

Bright, Michael. *Changing Ecosystems*. Chicago, IL: Heinemann Library, 2009.

Calhoun, Yael, ed. *Conservation* (Environmental Issues). New York, NY: Chelsea House, 2005.

Daintith, John, and Jill Bailey, eds. *The Facts On File Dictionary of Ecology and the Environment*. New York, NY: Facts On File, 2003.

Dupler, Douglas. *Conserving the Environment* (Opposing Viewpoints). Farmington Hills, MI: Greenhaven Press, 2006.

Eason, Sarah. *Ecology*. Tucson, AZ: Brown Bear, 2010.

Egendorf, Laura K. *The Environment* (Opposing Viewpoints). Farmington Hills, MI: Greenhaven Press, 2004.

Gibson, J. Phil., and Terri R. Gibson. *Plant Ecology*. Philadelphia, PA: Chelsea House, 2006.

Gore, Al. *An Inconvenient Truth: The Planetary Emergency of Global Warming and What We Can Do About It*. New York, NY: Rodale, Inc., 2006.

Latham, Donna. *Ecology*. Chicago, IL: Raintree, 2009.

Levete, Sarah. *Rot and Decay: A Story of Death, Scavengers, and Recycling* (Let's Explore Science). Vero Beach, FL: Rourke Publishing, 2007.

Orr, David W. *Earth in Mind: On Education, Environment, and the Human Prospect*. Rev. ed. Washington, DC: Island Press, 2004.

Spilsbury, Louise. *A Sustainable Future: Saving and Recycling Resources*. Chicago, IL: Raintree, 2006.

INDEX

ABOUT THE AUTHOR

Janice VanCleave is a former award-winning science teacher who now spends her time writing and giving hands-on science workshops. She is the author of more than forty children's science books.

Designer: Nicole Russo; Editor: Nicholas Croce

All photos by Cindy Reiman, assisted by Karen Huang.